INSTINCT TO RUIN

INSTINCT TO RUIN

poems by L Mathis

To:

My, and all of my friends' suicides
that did not happen.

And to the shit that almost killed us &
some days still feels like it might:

This is NOT for you.
Every laugh is in spite of you.
Every poem is an assurance that you did not win.

To unravel a torment you must begin somewhere.
Louise Bourgeois

I study my reflection and whisper,

I am afraid of what it means to be loved by you.
I am terrified of your instinct to ruin.

If There's A Way
Out I'll Take It

I want to talk
about what happened
without mentioning
how much it hurt.

There has to be a way.

To care for the wounds
without re-opening them.
To name the pain
without inviting it back into me.

The Poems Haunt
Not The People

I don't think they understand
how difficult it is for the poet to forget.
There is no shoving your skeletons
back into your chest after you have
paraded them around in poems.
Strangers own books with you
in them. They have words
to describe how you touch.

Once writing felt like letting go,
but now it feels like sitting in a bath for hours,
stuck in my own dirt.

Why is there still more pain to sift through?

the pain of reliving
of having a name for what happened
of marking moments as before and after
of explaining to new partners why my body stiffens
someone else with his name,
the dislike I form just by knowing it's his
of questioning if my friends are capable of the same
of quizzing myself on whether or not I could have
done more

Is it not enough that it happened?

High Water

After Fatimah Asghar, after Jan Beatty

We don't talk in the office but I know how your desk
feels against my cheek

& I know how many steps it takes to get from your
room to the front door
but the bed is soft & the moon is out & I need a ride to
work in the morning

& my silence puddles at my feet & my friend says I am
lucky I have a way to not to be carded & your cruelty is
a river I am too tired to dam

& if I close my eyes when you touch me I can almost
not feel you
& if I make myself very still I can almost imagine
myself unborn

& when you put your hand on my thigh in public a
flood of *no* streams through my ears
& I imagine the ocean swallowing me without remorse

& servers giggle at the pairing of your bald head and
my child's frown when we are out to dinner
       & I wonder if they will give me a ride home

& we are in the first course when I hear water rushing
towards the windows of the restaurant & steadily I
ask for another bottle of wine

& you offer me some of your salad
                & I question if the bathroom window
                could be crawled out of

& the wave is pouring under the door
& I lick my plate clean
& the tips of my hair are dripping down my chest & I
swear the sea is shaking with laughter & water rises
above my head

&

                I do not hold my breath

The Abuser Sleeps Soundly

There is probably a clear view of the Pacific ocean
from his new apartment,
just waves for him to look at he sips his post-work
beer,
musing to himself, *This is my kingdom. Mine. Mine.
Mine.*
The blue of it, boundless and still,
he will reach out his hand
and wish there was more to take.

Maybe there is a new 19 year-old shaking in his
passenger seat.
Maybe he really treats her right,
always making sure she is at least *half* awake
before slipping into her.

Maybe when he recounts my *LEAVE ME ALONE*s,
he laughs and laughs.
Maybe my name is an apartment of laughter to him,
the walls built of tender memories and
strong, long-lasting male entitlement.

While his name remains a glass chip
that makes me spit up blood
each time I swallow it.

I shrug off my body

and it drops lifeless on the table

during a game of poker.

Take it.

I don't want it anymore.

And That's It

All these dudes want to fuck me
and then forget me.

They like having me there when they feel like it.

Like to text me late at night when they are bored
saying, *Just thinking about you.*

They all want to wipe their drool on me,
then go to sleep. To them, I am just flesh.
Just a place to die for the night.
And that's it. That's it.

The Safe Space

To anyone who stopped going to shows
to avoid someone who hurt them

Someone in our safe and inclusive scene
is outed as an abuser and everyone claims
to not have believed him capable.

Meanwhile my mouth foams
with the times I said his name
and everyone shrugged.

The stories I told
and they told and
she told and he told
were not enough.
They lacked punch or were just drama.

Until the space closed
two years later because of his behavior.
Then suddenly it was *I never saw it coming!*

Ask me why my mouth
does not hang open in shock.

But this was not news.
It's not like the warning signs weren't there.
People just refused to look at them.

When they say bridges will be burned
if you dare tell anyone,
turn your tongue into a match.
Leave their home ash.

What He Tells His Friends
While I'm In The Bathroom

I'm looking for someone
made of smoke,
with no fight in them.
No teeth no tongue,
just an emptiness
waiting to be filled.

The type that has a handful of matches
but can only think of setting themselves on fire.
The kind that's so tired they'll leave the last
of their burning with you.

My Text To Him Days Later
After He Sends A 2 AM *WYD?*

You think that the fire smell in my hair
speaks of some ruin that will make your job easy?
That you have others to thank
for emptying me for you?
Don't you know I lick ash off my fingers,
longing for another just like you to set fire to?

One Year Later He Emails Me, *You're Finally Legal Now! Haha Also I'm Sorry*

Keep your chewed-up bubble gum of an apology
to yourself. No one wants it.

Alone in my bedroom I am holy.
Alone in my bedroom I am anyone I want to be.

In all the poems, I write myself back into safety.
In them, no one can touch me.

His hands go back into his pockets.
My door remains locked.
My phone never holds his number.
His name becomes a movement
my tongue never learns.

A slight of my fingers on the *Delete* button
hanging above his careless words
and he is gone.

Our introduction, incense ash on my dresser.
One sigh and the air devours him.

Bless the crazy femme.
For how much they endure silently.
For the survival game they
play against their heads
every day. For the hurt in them
that wants to swallow the softness.
May they know comfort in their bodies.
May their heads not win and the world be theirs.

They've Cast Me
In The Movie Of My Life
As Myself

and keep trying to write me happy.

They say,

We want to make relatable characters.
People don't pay for stories
that make them uncomfortable.

I say,

Do what you want
but the scenes people will talk about
are when the soundtrack is swelling
and the audience is watching through their fingers
as I flick matches off my tongue and say,

You want to see a trick?
Watch how I can make myself burn,
then dance on my ashes like it's nothing.
Like I was born of burning.
Like this is every day.

My Craziness Gets Cold One Night

So it sets the house on fire.

None of the neighbors
claim to have smelled
the burning.

The next day the
house is rebuilt. Resold.

The new owners talk about
how well the walls of their
home carry warmth
while next door
a neighbor carefully brushes
ash off their window.

This Is How It Goes No Matter Which City I'm In

When my sister asks me how I am doing
and I say, *I still have to adjust,*
what I mean is, it's been hard.

What I mean is, whenever I think I know
loneliness, it comes to me with a softer voice.
What I mean is, it is a lot easier to stay in bed
when there are fewer people asking where I've been.
And every time I want to call a friend
to ask for help I remember that everyone
has their own wounds to tend to.
What I mean is,
I know how worry can eat up a day.

When she asks me if I am happy here
and I say, *I like it, sure,*
what I mean is,
I am becoming a surer version of myself
but I don't know how many times I will sob
in a parking lot before this growing is over.

What I mean is, I'm writing poems about suicide
in a place with more trees.

My Mental Illness Is Mansplained To Me, Again

There is always a man
eager to explain my mental illness to me.
Somehow, every soft confession of my crazy
that I hand them turns into them
pulling out pieces of themselves
to show me how I should really feel.

Men tell their friends
about my impulsive decision-making
and how I get them more
than anyone they've ever met,
but leave out my staring off in silence for hours
and the self-inflicted bruises on my cheeks.
None of them want to acknowledge a crazy
they can't cure.

Truth is, they love me best
with my lipstick perfectly applied
and my sickness only creeping out
when they need a little excitement.
They don't want me dirty,
having not left my bed for days.
Not diseased. Not real.

So they invite me over when they need a pick-me-up
but don't answer my calls during breakdowns.

They tell me I look beautiful when I'm crying
then stick their hands in-between my legs.

And every time I go quiet, they mistake my silence
for listening to them attentively.

These men love my good dead hollow.
It means less personality for them to force out.

This hurting is
the only part of me
that has ever been mine.

Only Of Water

Late at night, I chew on my nails
and swallow the pieces I tear off
instead of spitting them out.
All I want is to fill myself
with something.

This is the person my loneliness
has made me into. Crying at 3 a.m.,
I try to call friends but have forgotten
all of their names. I spend months ignoring
my mother's calls then stare at my phone,
waiting for her name to buzz on my screen.
The screen stays grey.

In June, I dreamt only of water.
Waves snuck into my childhood bedroom
and took all my belongings with them.

An ocean spread between my friends and I
but none of us built boats to cross it.
A waterfall rose above me and I
lifted my head,
opened my mouth,
and swallowed.

My Body Gets An Illness That Is Not Invisible

When the skin infection comes,
so do the calls asking if I am okay.
Finally I get a sickness that makes
others believe I deserve to see a doctor.

They see my angry gapes of skin
and shudder. I can only stare at the wreckage.

It does not surprise me
to see my body destroying itself.
I have quietly lived with it happening
to my head for almost ten years.

I Come Out To My Mother As Crazy

and she asks me if I've been sleeping enough
or eating right.

I come out to her on accident.
We are in the car, driving to some small
Southern California beach town,
when she makes a comment about the sorts of people
who kill themselves.

I feel some wound in me being ripped open
as I think about being 16, or 8, or 21,
or any age that I was in a swinging match
with death and almost didn't win.

I list the years to her.
I do not mention the bruises
she has seen me inflict upon myself.
I do not mention the weeks she saw me spend in bed.
I say nothing of poetry.

And she says, *Well this is a surprise.*

I come out to my mother as crazy
and she asks why I am not embarrassed
telling people this.
And how many friends I have lost because
I am open about what is in my head.

I come out to my mother as crazy
and she tries to will me invisible again.
Says, *Things were easier before I knew about this.*

Because now when she sees me in a fight with myself
and laughs, it is not a question of her not knowing.
But not caring.

I am constantly in mourning.
There is always an old self
I am laying to rest.

My House Is On Fire

In a dream, my younger brother and I go
to our childhood home
looking for something we lost.
But all we find is another place we no longer belong.
Instead of answers we are filled with the sense
that something we never thought to give name to
because we assumed it would always be with us,
that it was in-fact a part of us, is gone.

Stars of Nothing

We stare out car windows
and pretend we are in a movie.
We make up soundtracks in our heads.
We want so badly to be important, but
there is nothing special about our lives.
We linger in parking lots because
we've got nothing better to do;
we go on trips to towns 45 minutes away
and think ourselves cool.

These moments are the best we've got.
They're nothing remarkable,
but look how gently we cradle them in our hands.
Look how much we love them
just because they're ours.

My Obituary Reads

She
or,
They
Or no, just
Dead Thing.

This Dead Thing is too long gone to be named
and who are we to say what it was
when we can only certainly say what it is now—
Something lost, soft and not breathing.

I hope in death my body can finally just be a body.
I want to take my gender under ground with me.

And if they misgender me
at least it will be the last time,
and I will not be there to hear it.
Leave others the job of cataloguing
a home that could not figure out
how to heat itself.

I Write This Poem To Re-enter Gender

They are a soft breeze made stale
in the back of a cab.
A wave crashed tired on the shore,
sighing as it is pulled back to sea.

They bounce between pronouns in their head.
Change their name six times in a conversation
and tell no one.

They are daughter at dinner time.
Miss to shop strangers.

But in their bed, they are a melting of wax.
In candlelight skin looks genderless.

They are whoever they want to be.

We are in love and sometimes
this is enough to quiet everything.

But sometimes it is
the reason for the noise.
Sometimes it is so loud
it gives me a headache.

This Is Surviving

We ride our bikes at night.
Leave the house when no one is around.
Make mediocre spaghetti at 10 p.m.

These nights are not always easy.
Often we spend them surviving,
but we are surviving.
We are still here.

We get up in the morning happy
to see each other alive
and I am thankful
for all of the times you have
unclenched my hands
or tucked me into bed
after I suffered a beating
from myself.

You know I would do
the same for you.

When The Friends You Thought Would Always Stay Together Break Up

I forgot that love isn't always a thing that dies.
Sometimes, it shifts.

It grows a face you don't recognize
until suddenly you're not sure how to hold it.
It still sits across from you at the dinner table
with all your ugly kept like a pearl under its tongue
but can no longer hold a conversation with you
without breaking eye contact.

Love doesn't always demand a funeral be held for it.
Or change its number and refuse to see you.
Sometimes it still shares a bed with you
and eats the dinner you cook,
but won't offer to help with the dishes.

Sometimes, it will drive away without leaving a note
for the tenth time
and you'll know exactly where it's going
but be too tired and uncertain to try to stop it.

On The Bus To Your Mom's
To Collect My Things
I Tell Myself This

Your heartbreak is not
the most important event in the world.
Still there are people getting up to start their days,
driving to work, making dinner.
You think your pain is so loud
that it could stop traffic.

But know that there is a healing in your insignificance.
Your missing them will not stop the highway buzz
outside the window.

And so?

Isn't there satisfaction in knowing
they are not the world?
You look for their face everywhere,
but no one else sees it.

Some days you will feel like the ocean.
Others you will feel like you are drowning in it.

After We Shoot A Breakdown
In The Movie Of My Life

The director pulls me aside and says they are
thinking of rewriting the script.
Our original plan was to stay as true to real life
 as possible but we think it's missing something.

I am exhausted.
We just filmed the part
where I pull out my hair and punch myself in the
face as my mother watches.

Like what? I ask.

It's just.
We know you're telling the truth
when you say this stuff happened.
But we don't know if the audience
will be convinced.

We think we need to add something
to the story to make you behaving like this believable.

I touch at my bruised peach of a cheek
self-consciously as they continue.

No one runs out into the street just because.
Or cuts off all their friends out of boredom.
There's got to be a reason.

We need to write a scene in that explains this whole thing. It's not enough to say that your head works like that. It's not realistic to say that you'd destroy everything around you just because you can.

Just Because I Can

When I'm angry I'll do anything
to prove that I'm still in control.
Sneak upstairs and drink all of the whiskey.
Bang my head on a corner
until there's a screaming bump
on my forehead for me to try and hide
once I'm calm again.
Run into the street at 3 a.m. just because I can.

Because I want to say,
Look at this ruin
and my two guilty hands.
All of my mess belongs to me.
There is nothing left for anyone to pick at.

When It Comes Down To It

I don't want sympathy
or pity. Don't want a knock
on the bathroom door
asking if I am okay.

I only want to pick
a fight with myself and see
if I can survive.

The Self-Portrait

Swallowing glass chips to stay interesting.
Keeping my insides cut so at least something
pours out when I open my mouth.

Spitting up blood. Calling it poetry. Calling it
performance.
Calling it everything but what it really is:
Self-deprecation for the sake of humility.
Self-dissolution to keep them guessing.

Playing the same game until it stops becoming one.

Here are some jokes I've made so many times
I've forgotten the punchlines:
Texting late at night, check.
Getting thin out of unintentional neglect, check.

This isn't a way to grow up, but what else is there?
Nice house? Nice car? Nice girl?

Wait. Didn't you used to be a nice girl?
Let's try this again.

Nice girl. Nice girls don't stay out late.
They don't forget their friends.
They don't lie in the street and call it therapy.

Nice girl. What happened to her?

Killed her. Cursed her.
Pushed her aside and cared for poetry.
Gave in and grew into something scalier, hungrier.

Nice girl. Why don't you call her up again?
Ask her how she's been?

Ah, but where's the fun in that?

My loneliness is a sea
and I have forgotten how to swim.

Think I'm Doing Fine

You ask what I have done with my life.
Why I am 23 with so many unfinished selves.
So many futures I could not commit to.
But you don't know how much of my time
has been spent keeping myself alive.

Lac Guidon

There is a poem about forgiveness I have
been trying to write, but don't know how to.
So instead I talk about the wild blueberry
patch in my grandmother's backyard.

How she spent the summer in the country watering
them,
picking them, making them into jam.
How she would hum softly under her breath in
French.

After her 81st birthday, the home was too much work
for her to maintain alone so her son sold it to
a young couple who wanted to visit the country on
weekends.
The night she put the keys in the couples' hands,
she fell asleep listening to soft French songs
and not humming along.

By the time she was 82, the blueberry patch
was overgrown; untended to, unloved.
She swore off blueberries for most of that Summer,
but one day in July,
she took the bus to the grocery store,
and bought three bushels of them.

That afternoon, she sang loudly
as she filled the counters with
fresh-baked blueberry pies.
I found her at night with a slice in hand
and a smile on her face.

She offered one to me as she said,

*This is how to move on. This is how you mourn
what you loved and forgive yourself for losing it.*

Every Goodbye Is
A Soft Recognition of Loss

We cross the street without looking.
Send bold texts when we're sober.

This loss is so familiar
we have given it a name, a toothbrush,
its own drawer in our dressers.

In afternoon quiet
we study tree shadows
lengthening on brick buildings.

Make a pact with the sunset to fade out beautifully.
These little exercises we run through
to prepare ourselves for death.

Call Me Any Time Of Night
for Matthew

It is three years into our friendship before I see you
cry.
It is while eating a fried chicken sandwich.
Later, when we meet up with our other friends,
you joke that you cried earlier because of how good
the food was.

All of my friends have hidden pains
that they cannot articulate.
I love them enough to want to
carve them open and freeze whatever
hurts them in poems.

Yet I still don't know
how to call them when I've been crying
for three days and can't stop.

We are friends for three years when you tell me
that things are getting bad and you're scared.

I love you enough then to want to stop it all-
the passing cars, the pedestrians,
and all of the noise humming on the street.
I want to make some grand gesture
to show you that I'm here.

Instead I nod.

I know there is no real way to stop the noise.
But I want you to know that I hear it all too.

The Depression Gets Real With Me

We are breaking you apart
to see if you are strong enough.
No. *Patient* enough.
No. *Hopeful* enough.

No.

We are peeling you apart bit by bit
because it is fun to do so.
Because this is just how it is.

There is no satisfying answer.
Nothing you did to deserve this brain
and this fear and us.

But here we are.
All yours and refusing to leave.

We are breaking you open because your childhood
is somewhere too deep to touch
and it's going to open its hungry jaws
to swallow you with or without us.

This isn't about reason.

This is about seeing how many times you can
choke on hope and still ask for another spoonful.

This is about taking away everything you rely on
and watching you scramble to new way to live.

We are giving you all of this aching
 to see what you can do with it.

On Heavy Days I Carry This

My tongue is now too thick with voice
to be swallowed easily.

You think me weak?
I have been making survival plans
in my journal since I was 15 years old.

My hand is still on the doorknob feeling for heat
but I am no longer ready to shatter the nearest
window and jump.

I am not here to hide.
I am here to find the flames and put them out.

Instead of Re-downloading Tinder
I Write This Poem

The loneliness hits when it hits.
There's not much you can do to turn
the white noise of it down.
Your ghosts don't care that you've hopped
to another coast.
They've got nothing on their plate
besides haunting you.

Read a book.
Steam your insecurities to death in the shower.
Log off. Don't hit send.
Force yourself to take a nap
before ending all of your relationships.

Tonight doesn't have to be the night
you solve everything.

Now I Know

Stability doesn't necessarily mean happiness.
It's not a great light bathing you each morning.

It is quieter. Softer.
Now I awake in my body
and my first thought is not to leave it.

Thank You

My friends, for your endless tenderness. I carry your kindness with me in everything I do.

Rivka, for editing this book with me and helping me shape so much of it. You bring out the softest parts of me.

Ben, for moving me across the country and endlessly supporting my work.

Rosie, Rachel, Kiki, Lauren, my readers.

Dianna, for the beautiful painting.

Clarissa, for scanning the cover.

Clementine and Where Are You Press, for giving my first book a home.

And, *to anyone who has supported me, cared about my art, housed me, fed me, loved me,* you allow me to view vulnerability as a gift and remind me of the importance of sharing. Thank you.

Previously Appeared In

After We Shoot A Breakdown In The Movie of My Life and *They Write My Obituary* appeared in Radar Production's GLOW.

They've Cast Me In The Movie of My Life As Myself and *Just Because I Can*, appeared in Polyester Magazine.

Versions of *Only of Water, This Is How It Goes No Matter Which City I'm In,* and *This Is Surviving* appeared in the chapbook *and the noise does not stop...*

Versions of *And That's It* and *The Self-Portrait* appeared in the chapbook *Bigger Bolder Less Pathetic.*

About The Author

L Mathis is an artist, writer, and musician from California. They are the author of chapbooks *and the noise does not stop...* and *Bigger Bolder Less Pathetic*. This is their second full-length collection of poems. Their first is available through Where Are You Press. They currently live in Philadelphia.

Made in the USA
San Bernardino, CA
18 December 2019

61979495R00046